US CAVES OF THE WORLD ™

Qumran Caves
Hiding Place for the Dead Sea Scrolls

Brad Burnham

The Rosen Publishing Group's
PowerKids Press™

For John and Jane

Published in 2003 by The Rosen Publishing Group, Inc.
29 East 21st Street, New York, NY 10010

First Edition

Editor: Nancy MacDonell Smith
Book design: Michael J. Caroleo and Michael de Guzman

Photo Credits: Cover, title page © Charles & Joette Lenars/CORBIS; p. 4 by Nick Sciacca; pp. 7, 8, 11, 12 © Richard T. Nowitz/CORBIS; p. 15 © PhotoZion.com/John Theodor; p. 16 © AP/Wide World Photos; p. 19 © David Rubinger/CORBIS; p. 20 © Bettmann/CORBIS.

Burnham, Brad.
   Qumran caves : hiding place for the Dead Sea scrolls / Brad Burnham.— 1st ed.
p. cm. — (Famous caves of the world)
Includes index.
Summary: Examines the formation of the caves in the ancient village of Qumran in present-day Israel, the discovery of the Dead Sea scrolls and other artifacts hidden in the caves, and what the archaeological findings reveal about the lives of the people who lived in ancient Qumran.
   ISBN 0-8239-6259-8 (library binding)
   1. Qumran Site (West Bank)—Juvenile literature. 2. Dead Sea scrolls—Juvenile literature. 3. Excavations (Archaeology)—West Bank—Qumran Site—Juvenile literature. [1. Qumran Site (West Bank) 2. Caves. 3. Dead Sea scrolls. 4. Excavations (Archaeology) 5. Archaeology.] I. Title. II. Series.
   DS110.Q8B87 2002
   956.95'2—dc21

                                    2001007775

Manufactured in the United States of America

Contents

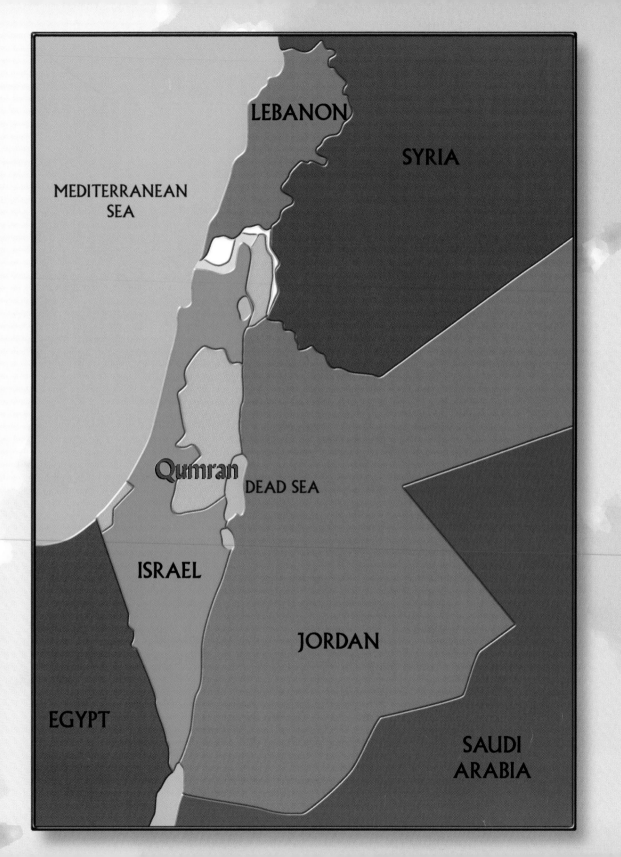

A Shepherd's Discovery

About 2,000 years ago, a group of people called the **Essenes** used some caves as a hiding place for their treasures. The Essenes lived in a town called Qumran, located in the **Middle East**. The caves were such a good hiding place that it wasn't until 1947 that someone found them again. That year, a young shepherd named Muhammed Adh-Dhib found one of the Essenes' caves while he was looking for one of his goats. Adh-Dhib was a member of a **nomadic** tribe that was camped nearby. Adh-Dhib scrambled inside the cave and found clay jars that contained rolls of paper with writing on them. He had made a very important discovery. He had found the Dead Sea Scrolls. This was one of the greatest discoveries of the twentieth century.

The Qumran caves are located near the shores of the Dead Sea, in what is now called the country of Israel.

What the Dead Sea Scrolls Are

The **scrolls** that Adh-Dhib found in the cave were written mostly in three languages. The languages are Hebrew, Aramaic, and Greek. Aramaic is an **ancient** language that was spoken during the time of Jesus Christ.

The scrolls act as history books for **scholars** who want to learn about the lives and religions of people who lived in Qumran 2,000 years ago. Some of the writings are about the laws they had for living in their community. Other writings are prayers. Many of the religious writings are about parts of the Hebrew Bible, which is called the Torah. These writings show that the religion of the Essenes was similar to that of both modern-day **Jews** and modern-day **Christians**.

Scholars have worked for 40 years to understand the Dead Sea Scrolls. Their findings were finally published in 2001.

More Cave Discoveries

In 1952, another cave was found that contained pieces of the Dead Sea Scrolls. The discovery of the second cave started a hunt for even more caves that might contain scrolls.

People searched the area around Qumran for many years to find more caves and more treasures. The searchers found about 40 caves that contained **artifacts** left behind by the people who had used them. More scrolls were found in 11 of these caves. The artifacts in the caves also included leather, **manuscripts**, **pottery**, pieces of wood, and scraps of food. More than 800 complete manuscripts and 10,000 pieces of incomplete manuscripts were found altogether. It took many years to put together the pieces of the scrolls.

The openings in the rock are all different entrances to Qumran caves. There may still be more caves to find.

Holes in the Rock

The caves near the Dead Sea are made of a kind of rock called **limestone**. The caves were formed when water ate away at the limestone. This took place over millions of years.

Water can create caves of all different shapes and sizes. Many of the caves near Qumran were small, but they were big enough for people to stand in and use for storage spaces.

Caves can change over time, though. The openings of caves can be sealed off by rock slides. Sometimes rock slides can cause a whole cave to fall in. Scientists have **excavated** some of the caves near Qumran that did fall in over time. There may still be more caves and more undiscovered scrolls buried in the rock near Qumran.

This photograph was taken in one of the caves that contained the Dead Sea Scrolls. As you can see, the cave is not very large.

The People of Qumran

People lived in the town of Qumran from about 150 B.C. to 68 A.D. Scientists believe that Qumran was home to a group of Essene **monks**. The monks lived in Qumran but used the nearby caves as places of prayer and for the storage of their valuables.

In 31 B.C., there was an earthquake and a fire in Qumran. The monks left the town but returned soon after. They left Qumran again in about 68 A.D., because the town was **invaded**. The monks left the scrolls in the nearby caves for safekeeping, but no one ever came back to get them. No one ever lived in Qumran again. The town was in **ruins**. The scrolls remained hidden until 1947, when Adh-Dhib discovered them.

Today ruins are all that is left of the town of Qumran. In ancient times the town was the center of the Essene community.

Protecting Valuable Words

The scrolls that the monks hid had laws, songs, poems, and religious texts written on them. The monks wanted the scrolls to last for a long time, so they made them well and carefully hid them away.

The monks made some of the scrolls and manuscripts from parchment, a kind of animal skin that was stitched together to make long rolls. After they wrote on the parchment, they rolled it up, tied it with leather straps, and placed it in clay jars. Other kinds of scrolls and manuscripts were made of papyrus. Papyrus was an early type of paper made from a tall grass of the same name. The scrolls and manuscripts lasted for so long because the monks stored them in the dry caves.

The Dead Sea Scrolls were stored in these clay jars. As long as parchment and papyrus stay dry, they can last for many thousands of years.

Scientists at Work

One of the scientists who explored the area around Qumran for more evidence of the Essenes was Roland de Vaux. He was a famous **archaeologist**. Archaeologists searched the caves and the ruins of the town of Qumran. They wanted to find artifacts left by the people who wrote the Dead Sea Scrolls and **evidence** of why the scrolls were hidden in the caves. In the ruins of the town, archaeologists have found a pottery workshop, fireplaces, and a large dining hall.

Searching for evidence is just the first part of archaeological work. After the archaeologists collect the artifacts, they use them to figure out what life was like at the time the artifacts were used.

An archaeologist searches for artifacts left by the Essenes. The artifacts at Qumran help us to understand how the monks lived and what they believed. **17**

Learning from the Clues

Scientists from around the world have been studying the clues in the artifacts from the Qumran caves and the surrounding area for more than 50 years. Much has been learned about the Dead Sea Scrolls and what they mean to people today. The scrolls describe the beginnings of the religions of Judaism and Christianity. The scrolls have been published in a book so that everyone can read about them. The book is called *Discoveries in the Judean Desert*. Judea was the ancient name for this part of modern-day Israel.

There are still many mysteries about the Dead Sea Scrolls. Even when the scrolls and manuscripts are complete, scholars will not agree about either the meanings of the writings or who wrote them.

Many of the Dead Sea Scrolls are in such tiny pieces that scholars have a hard time figuring out how to put them together.

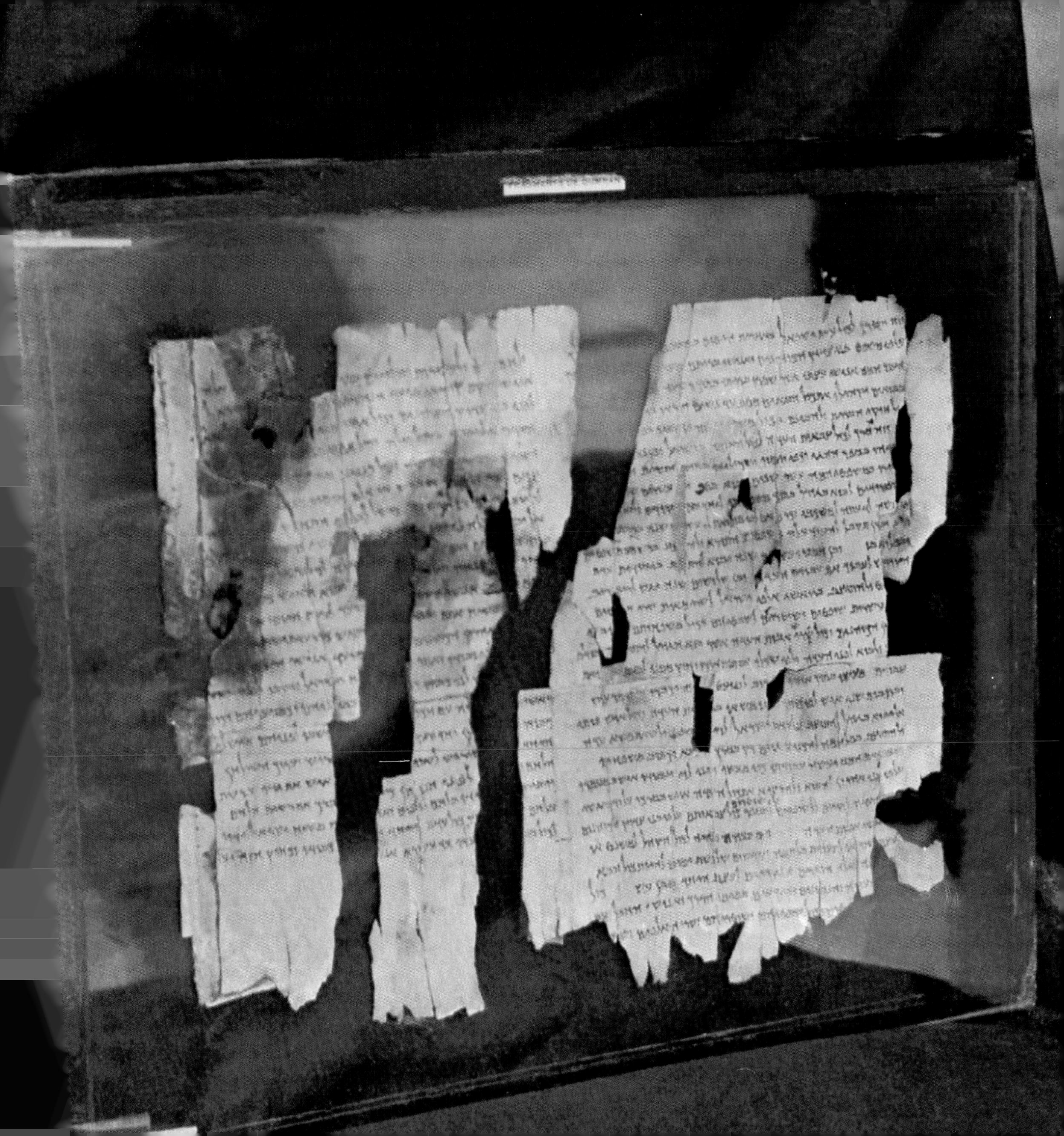

Missing Scrolls?

Ever since the discovery of the first scrolls, there have been stories of missing scrolls. Scrolls might have been found in caves near Qumran before 1947 and sold before anyone knew how important they were. Dead Sea Scrolls could also have been found in caves that were not explored by scientists. These scrolls could have been bought by people and put away for safekeeping.

Over the years, scrolls have appeared that could be part of the Dead Sea Scrolls. Scientists have studied these scrolls to see if they really are missing parts of the Dead Sea Scrolls. Any scrolls that do appear could help us to understand more about the people who wrote them. There are still many things we don't know about the Essenes.

This is a close-up of one of the pieces of the Dead Sea Scrolls. It describes the laws of the Essenes and includes a prayer of thanks.

Sharing the Discoveries

Some of the Dead Sea Scrolls and other artifacts found in the caves of Qumran have been put on **exhibit** for everyone to enjoy. The Shrine of the Book in Jerusalem, Israel, has an ongoing exhibit. The Library of Congress in the United States of America had a temporary exhibit on the Dead Sea Scrolls. Many items can still be seen on the Library of Congress's Web site.

The finding of the Dead Sea Scrolls by a shepherd was one of the world's greatest archaeological discoveries. The scrolls and other artifacts help us peek into the past and imagine the lives of the people who lived near the Qumran caves so long ago. The scrolls give us clues about what two of the world's most widely followed religions were like in ancient times.

Glossary

ancient (AYN-chent) Very old; from a long time ago.

archaeologist (ar-kee-AH-luh-jist) A scientist who studies how people lived long ago.

artifacts (AR-tih-fakts) Objects created or produced by humans.

Christians (KRIS-chunz) People who follow the teachings of Jesus Christ and the Bible.

Essenes (eh-SEENZ) A group of Jewish people who might have lived in Qumran.

evidence (EH-vih-dints) Facts that prove something.

excavated (EK-skuh-vayt-id) Dug up something that was buried or covered by rocks.

exhibit (ig-ZIH-bit) Objects or pictures set out for people to see.

invaded (in-VAYD-id) Attacked in order to conquer.

Jews (JEWZ) People who follow the teachings of the Torah.

limestone (LYM-stohn) A rock that is formed from shells and skeletons.

manuscripts (MAN-yoo-skripts) Books or articles that were written by hand.

Middle East (MID-uhl EEST) A region made up of Israel, Egypt, Syria, Jordan, Saudi Arabia, and other countries.

monks (MUNGKS) Men who are part of a religious order and who live by its rules.

nomadic (noh-MA-dik) Moving from place to place to find food and shelter.

pottery (PAH-tuh-ree) Pots and dishes that are made from baked clay.

ruins (ROO-inz) The remains of buildings, towns, or cities that have been destroyed.

scholars (SKAHL-erz) People who know a great deal about a subject.

scrolls (SKROHLZ) Rolls of paper or other material with writing on them.

Index

Web Sites

Due to the changing nature of Internet links, PowerKids Press has developed
an online list of Web sites related to the subject of this book. This site
is updated regularly. Please use this link to access the list:

www.powerkidslinks.com/fcow/qumran/